To Beth —

A Wolf
Stands Alone
in Water

I couldn't resist sending
you my "Wolf" book
because —

a wolf can hear a cloud pass —

Joe

A Wolf
Stands Alone
in Water

Joseph Zaccardi
2019

Poems by

Joseph Zaccardi

CW Books

ISBN: 9781625491596
LCCN: 2015955635

Published by CW Books
Poetry Editor: Kevin Walzer
Business Editor: Lori Jareo
P.O. Box 541106, Cincinnati, OH 45254-1106

Book design by Jeremy Thornton, www.jftdesign.com

Grateful acknowledgment is given to the editors of the following publications in which these poems originally appeared.

Spillway: "The End of Love," and "Infantryman (No Dog Tags)"

In Posse: "You Have Ten Minutes to Explain Infinity"

Squaw Valley Review: "Tied to Nothing"

Marin Poetry Center Anthology: "Ceremony," "Vessel," "Cutout,"

"Weather Forecast," "After Creation," "Pain Outside the Body," and "Little"

Reckless Writing, Chatter House Press: "1916," and "Lamb Wolf Farmer God You"

Schuylkill Valley Journal: "Schuylkill"

Poet Lore: "On the Outskirts"

Pedestal Magazine: "Duck's Nest"

California Quarterly: "Sacrifice," and "Yard"

in Memoriam

Jean Pumphrey

12.3.1931 – 8.5.2014

O my dear friend, it is idle to talk of what I feel —
I am stunned and this beginning to write makes
a beginning feeling within me.

Contents

THE SCALE THAT MEASURES OUR LIVES

A MAP OF QUESTIONS

PAIN IS ABOUT DAMAGE

THE WHEAT FIELD

Introduction

A Wolf Stands Alone in Water is about damage and repair. What is found here, to paraphrase William Carlos Williams, is an uncensored exploration of the human heart. Neither flinching from evil nor denying glimpses of the divine, Joseph Zaccardi guides the reader through visceral encounters with evils announced daily in the headlines (and the even darker evils hidden from newsprint and camera) to acknowledge, "In everything that holds light, there is room / for darkness."

Zaccardi explores moments of inexplicable pain and moments when the soul, like a god, "rests peacefully / on a hammock swagged to a walnut tree." He affirms mysteries of the ineffable, those moments transcending human understanding. "When nature has work to do, she changes / the most complex things to the most simple. She holds them / to herself and makes of the earth a map of questions."

In the pilgrimage between pain and healing, "Pain is about damage. / Healing is about repair." Even as it travels toward exile, the human heart seeks and acknowledges beauty — a rainbow bridge, a girl playing a lute, reflections rippling the water underneath and against the boat.

Grab hold. Hold on. Begin the journey.

– Yvonne Postelle

A Kind of Surrender

This morning the last bloom
on the wisteria fell away.
Why is it I close my eyes to music
and open them when there's a storm?

Pain Outside the Body

You Have Ten Minutes to Explain Infinity

First minute: a butterfly.

Second minute: petrified wood.

Third minute: the molten core of the earth.

Fourth minute: a leviathan.

Fifth minute: the fossil of a fern.

Sixth minute: a dead star.

Seventh minute: conception.

Eighth minute: a newborn.

Ninth minute: truth.

Tenth minute: a silkworm.

And when you meet God, you'll have ten minutes.
Explain: you didn't know.

Two Things

In a cemetery an old man
clacks two stones together
as he passes each grave marker.
Across the road, a woman sits
on her front porch and plays a flute
made from the tibia of an elk.
Occasionally, travelers pass
between the cemetery
and the clapboard house.
Where they are going
doesn't matter.

A Season

She lives on West Mountaintop Road;
the trees on either side of her house are like a sea.
Today, as she does every spring day,
she goes out for a walk, wades in the smells,
and calls to her dog, Sophie, who rolls
in the grass, chases anything that moves.
Back in the house, she soft-boils an egg
in its shell for three minutes, toasts one slice
of whole grain bread, opens a gift of mango jam.
Outside the clouds are distant, and the dog
is resting under blooms of weeping cherry.
The peonies are almost ready, the ants
feasting on their sweet nectar,
and the trees swell.

Edge

She would hold a peeled potato in one hand and use a paring knife in the other to cut the potato into quarter inch slices. One time I said to her, *You should use a cutting board to do that,* and under her breath I heard her say, *Oh shut up.* Another time she stood on a shaky kitchen chair to put up a curtain rod. I didn't say anything. I watched my mother, my elbows on the tabletop, my folded hands under my chin. I thought, if she falls I can help her up, and she would thank me. It was all she ever wanted from me.

Alyssum

My mother calls from her nursing home.
She says, Get me out of here. Her voice
is forceful. I say, What's wrong?
There were spiders lined up around
my bed last night, she says, they didn't
move. I held still until they went away.
I don't remember when or where they
had gone to. Not this, not this she says
to her undying self. There were white flies
in my garden and they hovered over
the sweet alyssum, and when I went out
to see them they left me, the ground
cover left me, and the yard was barren,
the fruit trees were barren. And where
everything had gone I do not know.
I could touch nothing and nothing
could touch me. And there was no place,
there was no place. Perhaps the gods,
she says, are jealous of death. They hold
you until you are still and then they leave
you because they do not care. Faith
does not prove anything. Why
won't you, she says? I say, I can't, let's talk
about this tomorrow. She hangs up on me.
Ten minutes later she calls again.
She asks, Are you all right? You're doing
too much, let the laundry go. I say
I'll see you tomorrow. She says, Good,
get some rest.

Pain Outside the Body

She used talcum on her face so that even her love for me did not show. When she died everything seemed so plain. She used to ask me what it was I was thinking. I could see her worry and would answer, Nothing. And she would say, No, there is something.

I once saw a man fall overboard into the sea. The ship steamed away at thirty knots. This is not a great speed. And the horizon looked to be a perfect circle. I was always at the center. And when the man who fell overboard was saved, I thought about myself.

Her body was still warm. I spoke to her in a soft voice, not wanting to wake her. With my hand I smoothed a few stray hairs from her forehead that always used to bother her. This one time they stayed perfectly in place.

Destiny

In the great book it says,
in the order of things, chaos
and tranquility are equal.
The body fills, then empties.
The body holds and is held.

Lock

Through the window is a room
and in the room two doors,
one to the closet and one
to the hallway; down the hallway,
on either side are stairs, both going
to the same room, called
the great room, with doors
to enter by and windows
for sunlight to come in, and if
they are open the wind can come
in too; and people can go in and out
through the doors, if the doors are
unlocked.

The Thing Lost

There's an old man puttering around in his garden.
He checks in on the marigolds, and on the crab apples
hanging about his head, talks to the oregano
in the herb bed, says something like, Up early
this morning, or Would you like to join the marinara
sauce simmering on the stove? This is a good garden
where an old man can mutter to himself. But then
he loses his way; now it seems to him he's on
a remarkable journey. He's looking for the lost door
to the back of his house. The harder he tries to find
this door, the more befuddled he becomes. The vinca
seem to conspire to trick him, as 'round and 'round
he goes along the border and fence line trying his best
to follow the sun like the sailors of old. For surely the sun
can find the back porch, and he remembers distinctly
the back porch leads to the back door. Can this old fellow
find his way out of the forest? Should he stay put,
as his father told him to do when he was a little boy,
and wait to be rescued? He stops then by the rosebush
that has the curious name of Mister Lincoln and watches
the translucent sky and listens to the cries of children
in other yards.

Yard

The end of summer is at hand. Peaches lie on the ground.
An old dog goes from backyard to backyard looking
for handouts. He finds some newspapers spread out
on a back porch open to the financial page. It's all about
ups and downs. He remembers an old bone and the time
he had with a dead squirrel. This dog has never known
a dead-end street — he travels in circles and has never
come close to going the same way to anywhere.
He lies down on the newspapers. He thinks about snow.

Speaking in Tongues

The clouds are gone, an autumn light
settles on the hills. Like a runner in trouble
I feel a vague urgency course through me.
My stepfather is dying of cancer.
I promise to be there when it happens,
to kneel in silence. The doctors have given him
a time, and my stepfather holds that time out
at arms length, feels it shrink and expand.
He sits in his chair, the feeding
tubes busy with pink and amber liquids.
Sometimes he talks about his dying
as something he could almost touch,
like sunlight streaming between stands of maple
or a star plucked from the dark and held
in a tight fist, something he can neither keep
nor let go. He says he wants to visit Loch Garman
one more time. Outside, his dogs bark
at the flutter of leaves or at a chipmunk running
through the just cut grass. The ordinary bares
such beauty.

Euphemism for Cancer: It's Probably Nothing

Life is about the expectation of the unexpected.
It is said no one can draw something that is alive

or that once lived, without in some sort becoming that life.
In ancient Chinese tradition to consume first the eyes

of a fish is to insure good fortune. Vision is not about what is seen,
it is what is hoped for. Hunger cannot be appeased, only delayed.

One body feeds on the body of another and so on.

In Time

Because the spring
is coiled too tight.
Because the battery is dead.
Because water got inside.
Because all the moving parts
have stopped. The watch that runs
like a clock is exact. The other is inexact
and runs five minutes behind every twenty-four hours;
loses a day every two hundred and eighty eight days.
Time running backward. The watch that runs fast
is ahead of the game, doesn't get stuck, is soundless
because it has no moving parts. The watch you check
before you arrive somewhere. The watch you glance at
mid-sentence. The watch that measures the pulse.
Watch of paralysis: to see, to view the body, the fatal, the fate.
Because all the parts have stopped. Because you didn't get there
soon enough. Because you were too late.

The Watcher

He has found the key
to the lock of universal questions and answers.
He is certain this will be big, but when watching
the eleven o'clock news that night, after seeing
all the usual stories, he is intrigued
by one item: apparently there'd been a cataclysmic
explosion on Arcturus, the Watcher, a star
of the first magnitude in the Boötes constellation.
He surmises that someone else has also found
the key to the lock of questions and has, without
public announcement, turned a latch and opened
the door to all the answers. Surprise,
said Arcturus. The way a star might collapse
in a fit of laughter. Surprise being the key
to all answers. He is an old man and feels
a bit smug now after being ignored, and decides
to keep the key in a place he is sure to forget
in no time.

Frustration

A man is out in his backyard digging a hole.
There is eagerness in the way he rams
the shovel into the hard clay soil with his right foot.
His wife calls from the kitchen window, Come in
to dinner. He ignores her. You're going to kill
yourself, leave it for tomorrow, she says. He wants
to get the root-ball of the tree into the hole before dark,
he wants to rip away the burlap casing. Fucking earth!
he screams. All over the neighborhood his shouts
can be heard, but he won't stop. There's a look
on his face like he wants to cry. But no one sees that.
He screams again.

Regression

My father curls his body into a fist. Perhaps
he dreams of being a worm embedded
in the earth, feeding on the decomposed
peel of an apple. His face quiets, his breathing
deepens. There's a song going on inside him.
In sleep the body grows frailer.

Heart Bone Hand

The old clock in the living room had to be rewound
every three days or else it would lose time.
The chestnut woodwork treated with tung oil
was buffed every three months with a soft cloth.
The hand woven rug in the center of the room
had to be taken outside each spring to be beaten
with a broom to release the dust among its fibers.
When the old couple who lived in this house
and who shared many years together in this living room
died, they were taken away and buried.
Now there is no more time to be lost, no woodwork
to feel the laying on of hands, nobody
to pummel the rug until satisfied.

Underneath

A worm having its way with the dead.
This is life. The breaking down and building up of the cell.
And this is death. A play where the worm is the victor.
How to stop this. Stop the worm. To prolong life,
take neither alcohol nor tobacco, nor take too seriously
the caresses of men. To prevent death, don't go to any play
where there's a cast. Brag when you're young. Lament
when you're old. Stay awake. Keep still. Hold on
to every night. The cock makes the loudest racket
in the morning. The worm is mute for a reason.

The Scale That Measures Our Lives

Another Eden

The snow has covered everything.
The garden is still there but softer,
the lawn chair and birdbath, the grass,
the straw stacked along the fence line,
the ivy that clings to the legs
of a Ming horse statue, the rake left on the ground,
prongs up, after the gathering. To walk
on this snow would be wrong, would change
almost everything.

Whales Sing to One Another

Because they know they are not alone.

Because this is natural. Because

it is not the order of the musical notes that attracts,

it is the variations. Music is about hunger, about composition.

The religious and the nonreligious

understand the power. To control the body,

control the sound inside the mind.

Catullus tells us a feast is more for the eyes than the belly.

And that love is an unphysical joining.

A *harmony,* not *harm* — the first word from Latin,

the second from the Middle English,

two words not altogether different.

The way starvation is not altogether different

from desire. The sounds come first

from the body.

Succor

There are bones in many places on and in the earth.
Some have calcified. Some have bleached
so white it's hard to believe they were once a part
of a living body. Some bones are scattered and charred,
even the most adept paleontologists cannot with any certainty
identify them. When nature has work to do, she changes
the most complex things to the most simple. She holds them
to herself and makes of the earth a map of questions.

After Creation

I once set a house on fire; it was abandoned and boarded up.
The neighborhood boys had already broken the glass panes
with stones, now covered with plywood. Things go badly for an old house;
this one was paintless, the clapboard siding a woodsy gray.
Black streaks bled through from the resin in the cedar
where the nails were hammered into the studs. I lit a match
in a hole where the utility box had been ripped out. The house filled
with smoke and seemed to come alive as it groaned and popped;
then flames shot out from both sides at once and the roof sagged,
and my eyes watered and I blinked to clear my vision. I had to turn
and run away. And if there were sirens, I would have remembered.
In every story there's a lie. Some call this a turn. Here's one:
I washed my face and hands when I got home and left
soot prints on the fancy guest towels my mother put out for show;
I used my father's lavender-laced aftershave to cover up my smell.
And here's some of the truth: I learned that day that water means life
and that fire is abstract; being thirteen years old, this seemed important.

Transmigration

A friend calls from a great distance. A satellite
connection. His voice comes from within his body.
Perhaps that is the soul showing itself. He tells me
things about the dailiness of his life, what his plans
are for the future; about the things that didn't work out.
His voice fills with questions. It is a good thing
the world is round, he says (drawing in and holding
his breath), for even if we lose our way, chances are,
we'll return to the same place over time. Yes,
the voice is the soul. How can I disagree with what he says?
I tell him tomorrow I'll buy a saw, a hammer, some nails,
and build something.

Cycle

I toss a sunflower onto the tides.
Face-up it returns to me, sloshing
at my feet. When I was six years old
I planted the seed of a sunflower
along a retaining wall in my

                    backyard.

The stalk grew to twice my height.
I have learned to accept tears
brought to me, learned about soil
and about salt.

Blessing

She scrubbed my back with a sea sponge,
bathed my chest, my arms and hands,
my legs and feet. Held the sponge out for me to take,
turned away slightly to give me privacy.
Then she poured buckets of warm seawater over me
as I sat on a nine-inch-high wooden stool.
Eyes closed, I felt the water course and trace
over my body, each part and crevice blessed.
And maybe she allowed herself to look upon me.
And maybe this one time I could feel
my own goodness and taste salt on my lips.
Though you wash yourself with niter and use
an abundance of soap, the stain of your guilt
is still there.

Shamed by the Innumerable Silence of Stars

To never let go is a terrible burden.
The heart that is unable to empty itself
breaks into ten thousand pieces.

It is cruel to confine a man who has nothing to do.
The righteous think of religion as a justification.

In nature there is more randomness than there is in a game
of chance. A mob is less predictable than a gangster.

Who can weigh the balance of a mountain?
I praise the cattle, which graze on spring greens,
because they believe the rancher loves them.

Memory is sometimes assisted by moonlight.
It is better to prefer memory to the calendar.

Breaking Bread

To eat with animals, you must break bones
with your teeth.
To eat at the table of the poor, you must put
your elbows on the table,
learn there will be no leftovers.
To eat at the table of the dispossessed,
you must learn the meaning of apportionment,
that the sweetest fruit is always out of reach,
why herbs pulled up by the roots can nourish you.
To eat at the table of the soldier, you have to practice
dying, learn to sleep with the dead.
To eat at the table of a widow, you have to learn
that bitter greens are best for healing.
To eat at the table of the lost child,
you have to understand emptiness.
To eat at the table of the powerful you must learn
the placement of silverware, the order of the courses;
learn that waste is a kind of victory.
To eat at the table of the farmer,
your hands must be thick with callouses,
your eyes full of hope and prayer.
To eat at the table of the gods, you must understand
they consume everything and nothing;
they do not need you.

Lamb Wolf Farmer God You

If you were a lamb, I would be your shepherd;
with my staff I would protect you from the wolves,
with my flute I would lull your fears.

If I were a wolf, I would rip out the lamb's throat,
feed on her buttery liver and sweet meat,
her entrails; let scavengers feast on what is left.

If you were a wolf, I would admire your cunning,
the way you trot with your muzzle close to the ground,
because you always hunger.

If I were a farmer, I would set traps laced with strychnine.
If I saw you near my flock I would shoot you with my shotgun.

If you were a farmer, I would be your sky-god and bring you soft wind
and gentle rains; a soil rich in nutrients, worms turning
to aerate the earth, then, because my mood changes,
I would bring you swarms of locusts, followed by unbearable heat
to sere and shrivel your crops — a seven years'-long drought.

If you were a god, you would rest peacefully
in a hammock swagged to a walnut tree.

I would let you be.

Sacrifice

Bees will not abandon their dead queen,
but after a time they will consume her body.
When cranes mate, they mate for life.
When one dies the other flies
over the open sea until it can fly no more.

In the time of the Yellow Emperor,
the eldest female child
would cut off parts of her body
and feed her parents small pieces of her flesh
until they were cured.

A Map of Questions

Little

If he had the sense he was born with but he did if he'd taken off
his doughboy uniform that a hostile band of whites demanded
but he didn't there in Blakely Georgia in that spring of 1919
when he arrived at the railroad station after the war and he said
these were the only clothes he had but they said well walk home
in your underwear but he didn't he wore that uniform for two weeks
he did and some folks said they didn't think it was right that a black
no less should parade around dressed up like a white hero no less
but he did the nerve they said when Private William Little was found
on the outskirts of town badly beaten when this doughboy veteran
was killed because he wouldn't and didn't doff the only clothes
he had and walk home in his underwear he wouldn't
he was wearing his uniform when found

1916

Who was burned alive that day in that year
a man untried un-convicted undressed by a mob
was bound to a stake in the ground then the crowd
had grown to two thousand and then another man poured
kerosene oil over him and afterwards no one would say
who did this other than to say he was an outsider come south
from Pennsylvania

I'm not going to tell you where this took place exactly
other than to say it took place and then they cut off his ears
his privates as souvenirs and then after torching him he let out a scream
that could be heard a mile away reported the Chicago Sentinel
then those who were a party to this damped down the flames
posed for snapshots and then they re-anointed him
with heating oil and then reignited him
now try to imagine afterwards the quietness
of this place

the unnamed trees facing sun shade growing long at their backs
it is hard to say in so many lines the truth is hard
to not give expression and then afterwards the throng swarmed
cutting away pieces of bone and hardened liver
from this colored man's corpse and then some later sold their mementoes
for as much as twenty-five cents

On the Outskirts

Denmark, South Carolina (1899)

I took the bird's-eye view he told the reporter
for the Bangor Maine newspaper because
partaking in lynching parties is disagreeable business
especially as it was dog-day hot and the mob
of men and boys argued over which of two trees
nearby to use then settled on a swaybacked oak
near a ditch near the crossroad of two train lines
going which-ways through Bamberg County and then
under the shade they lugged some railroad ties
across this ditch and the victim was made to stand there
while one of the eminent town leaders read from Leviticus
at which time the townspeople quieted a bit but then
some stamped their feet on the red-clay soil
because they wanted to catch the half-past twelve
to get back to their farms and homes and such
so a few local reporters showed them how an execution
ought to work in the regular way hanging then shooting
making this a well-arranged affair then when the rope
was made ready they pulled the ties from under this poor sort
and whilst he danced he was honeycombed with bullets
and some men scrubbed their hands with hoarhound leaves
against the stink of creosote and boys cheered
as the train hustled in sight and it turned out the lynched man
was innocent of an attempt to outrage a white woman
after the guilty man found in Georgia confessed

Hangman

Is there an L?

Yes, from the Phoenician for *ox-goad*.
The secret of L's sound is the lateral emission of breath.
The L soothes, the lull of the spiritual singer, the lullaby.

Hanged from a cottonwood tree, flourishing by a stream,
his skin is a beautiful black sheen, his eyes
slightly opened, his body without warmth.
This is the way the recalcitrant are taught,
someone wrote on the back of a dime-store postcard,
and on another, *This is the day the amaryllis belladonna bloomed.*

Is there a Y?

The forked letter. Yes, there is a Y. *The hook,* the crucifixion.
Glide the tongue into position below the palate to make the sound
of the vowel that follows.

She is hanging from the rafters of a sawmill, her ears cut off, hands cuffed
behind her back, her bare feet scraped the barn's upright post.
Spectators held kerosene lamps. That is why this lithograph seems out
of focus, because she swayed, because the yellow light moved.

Is there an N?

The nose acts as a sound box for the letter N, the tongue
set against the palate. The dental nasal, of all sounds,
is the least likely to change. The air trapped, then released,
the rope taut, the neck's connective tissues snapped.
The N is the *fish* on a hook.

This is the way we learn why the photographer holds
the lens open to gather in the seconds
of this falling body in light.

Is there a C?

Yes, and it is the unvoiced sibilant, as in *cider* and in *cycle,*
and redundant before *k,* as in *thick* and *clock.* It is the last sound
to leave the body, the *chill* in soul, the *chatter* in cold.

The chains dragged through the red mud
behind a stubborn mule; the mule dropped
in his tracks, the landscape arranged in furrows,
the heads of the cotton balls tan in this undulating heat.
In this way lessons are learned.

Is there an H?

The H, a *twisted hank of rope,* can lay claim to the expelling of breath;
its sound involves no other pronunciation. The initial H is spoken
in Germanic origins, as in *hunt* and *hook;* in some words
of Romance origin it is silent, as in *heir* and *honor*
but in others restored, as in *humble* and *humor.*

Are there no other letters? No. There are only the hanging bodies,
only these two gelatin silver print postcards with a low-grain appearance
because of their sensitivity to light. Oh yes, there was a windmill
in the background in the former, in the latter, bloodhounds;
dates and locations unknown.

All About It

The day's story the next day's story the story
busy downtown nighttime bustle another story
on a city sidewalk smack-dab on the concrete slab
a man sleeps stretched-out legs the story goes crossed hands
overlapped that's continued in tomorrow's story across his chest
a down-and-outer taking an overnighter catching a few
white starry rays not the same as the weekend story about comet watchers
while everyone else the suited the well heeled the tourist from middle this
and middle that that's the featured story moves aside for this guy
the story from the other day's story continues on page 53 section two
lying on unread day-old newspapers as several pigeons goose-step
around his laid-out presence peck at the inlaid pavers
scavenge for the stepped-on bugs eying the half-eaten
muffin bits splayed that's on another page on this vagabond's vest
where it does not matter where he lies on newsprint
in another story teens set fire to indigent see back page for whole story
placed after the advertisement insert perhaps a disbarred lawyer
or disgraced broker who's been binged by overwork who's been frayed
by overdrink comes to this lower life by anyone's scale back story
vagrant man dies in burn unit prosecutor says not hate crime
courts grant bail for under-aged suspects because they have good
families read the times the chronicle the tribune
in the moment this week's roundup in entertainment today

Unloved

In the beginning they were untouched.
In the beginning they were unsullied,
but in the end they were driven away.
Before them was only fire, before them
and behind them; it rose like bouquets
and made a wreath around them, so that
they stood in ash and breathed in ash,
and their eyes filled with this ash so that
it did blind them. And the flames leapt
and became not light but the end of light.
And because there was no water, not even
water enough for one tear, not even for
remorse, not even for regret, not even
for each other's eyes, they did wither.

Cutout

On the page a line of ink and in the line, blood.

Often what the line says wears a mask.

So the story goes; a father finds out that his son is gay.

In a calm voice, he calls for his son to come out to the barn.

There is straw on the compacted dirt floor, in the loft

bales of hay, and in the hay the movement of some small animals.

The father has his son turn away from him and has him kneel,

has him bow his head as though they were going to pray

together. Without another word he puts a shotgun to the boy's neck.

Then he walks away. Cutting reveals what has vanished,

a thing whose presence is its absence.

Weather Forecast

Today our father is giving us new names: my beautiful first son, my beautiful second son, he says, my beautiful daughter, my one and only beautiful daughter. This morning, which he calls today, there are no demons swirling around his head, his hair is full of flowers, his breath is sweet with words, his eyes are lucent. We sit in a circle, no trapdoors, measuring our breaths, keeping still with this gift of our new names. On another day, much like today, he summons us to the parlor, he shutters our windows, he deadbolts our doors. He scratches the walls with his screams, and his face is locked up in a spasm. He covers the room with his threats. We each choose a corner; we shield our bodies and use our arms, our frail arms. The hard part is waiting. We count the seconds left on this fuse that he has lit. It is evening, and it is coming close.

The End of Love

Daddy says it will not hurt. He says
to tell him if it does and he will stop.
He smells so good, the way cinnamon
bread smells when it is in the oven baking.
I tell him to stop because this does hurt,
and he does. He caresses my hair, he kisses
me on my forehead. It is as though a feather
has touched me and left a scar. He covers me
with my dancing-bear blanket and sits in the corner
on the floor. His head is in his hands, his shoulders
tremble. I can hear his deep breaths before
I fall asleep. Someday I will kiss him
on his forehead. He will not know
it is me. He will not know.

The Age of Majority

When he asked if he could smell my fingers, I wasn't surprised, I let him, right there at the crowded bar on Kuhio Avenue, where anyone could watch. He said he used to be a priest, and I said, *Tell me more*. He smelled my fingers; I could feel his breath, it was gentle, and I could smell the gin, the juniper, this poison he drank. Then he asked how old I was. I didn't answer, then said, *That's not important*. He looked sad; he looked like a priest secretly praying that I could be the one. Then he asked me what was the most twisted thing I'd ever done. He said, *Sexually*. And I watched him smelling my fingers, turning my hand over, then back again. I didn't think what he was doing was twisted, no way, but said that it was and he seemed pleased, he sighed, asked me if I wanted a drink, a highball, that's what he said, and I said if I had a drink he would have to let go of my hand and that I would leave him, maybe the way he left the church, because of the way he was, what he was. He said he left the priesthood because he could no longer believe, and I closed my hand, the way one would do to capture a lightning bug, to extinguish something, to save it, so that I could keep it forever inside me. Then I slid off the barstool, turned and walked away, down the stairs, across the street and went one block farther to Waikiki beach, all the while thinking about *A Star Is Born*, about Judy Garland when she sang, "The Man That Got Away," about James Mason, when he left their beachfront house and waded into the ocean and drowned, to save her the embarrassment, and how there was a kind of bravery to this act. Thinking about his alcoholism, the corrosive things that ate away at his spirit, the salt air, and the warmth of that night. I too tried to cross a frontier to another place, to become a being in an unexplored country. Then I felt someone near me. It was my priest, my Father, from the bar. He clung to me, he took me into his lungs, the smell of me; the smell of the ocean, rolling, lapping. He called me *my son*. And I caressed his white hair, my palm gliding over his waves. I lowered my eyes. I waited. I said *Do you want me?* A proposition — that what I do, I do for money, that underage meant nothing to me. I knew what I was doing to him. I knew he thought I wanted love, his love. And because I refused to drink with him, because I let him smell my fingers, he trusted me. The force of the son. He curled his arms around me, for a moment didn't breathe. Then he said, *Everything.* And I knew he was mine, under my control, and if asked to strip off his clothes and swim away from me, he would do it, he would go as far as he could, not turn back. I had him and he had me. I offered him my fingers, and he licked them, he rubbed them on his face, he could not let me go. He could not toss me to the stars. He wanted love and I wanted his ministering, wanted him and this time. Everything.

Thirteen

In the morning
he searched for answers
and found there were no answers.
And as easy as it was to turn a page
in a magazine, the easier it was to think
of his fragile body floating free;
and what about words, his poems,
already forgotten, already a back issue.

In the afternoon
he used his Sunday dress-up tie
to hang himself in the ill-lit hallway
at his junior high.
How did he get in, everyone wanted to know?
There were signs of depression.
There were the gay taunts
at school and in his neighborhood.

In the evening,
in the ocean, everything changes
and begins again.

Tied to Nothing

They beat him.
Because he was different they draped and tied his body
on a high ridge-fence. A passing mountain biker said he thought
what he saw was not human; thought he saw a scarecrow.
How quickly things change.

Sometimes you have to turn up the light to see
the darkness. They covered his eyes, covered his body.
The sun rising, the field fallow, the fence poles turned
lucent in this light. The prairie is beautiful.
The way a black and white film is vivid. And words
are unimportant in the execution of things.
Because there are blind spots.

The Paper Boy

Ryan was expelled from middle school.
His teachers, his classmates, the parents of his classmates,
railed against him. He carried the gay plague,
they said, and God is vengeful, they said.

There was a time when those afflicted with cancer
were shunned, turned away by friends, by family.
What is learned? What is passed along?
Fear, the bread and water that nourishes the present;
an immersion in the flood of everyday concerns;

a descent of sound. We know you're queer, people shouted
after him. He said, I'm just like anyone else with AIDS,
no matter how I got it.

Could this disease be spread through the ink of newsprint, they queried.
I am not paper. I am what you read each day, he answered.
What can be said that has not been written first; from Proverbs:
Show the sun with a lantern. So much happens in contraction.
Our souls shrivel from daily inhumanities.

The scale
that measures our lives,
neither black nor white,
is said to be gray.

The Field Is Never Fallow

for Polly Klaas 1981-1993

I sleep and cannot awaken. The tule fog
lifting in the wind, washing over the roadbed
near Cloverdale. Passenger cars and pick-up trucks pass by,
their windshields caught in the oncoming halogen glare.
Past barren fields, bare orchards.
Moving windows, wiper arms going
left to right, saying: *night sky, night sky,*
empty sky.

Everyone said I was beautiful.
Headlights going toward darkness, red tail-lights
recalling the distant. I rearrange the letters in *asleep*
and find the word *please*. I, who was once alive,
have come to my end. My mother cries,
I have a daughter out there without shoes.
I can hear my mother. How is it
I am dead, lying in an untilled field?

Come now, come now, let the storms
come, let the weather change.
Let the fruit trees go dormant,
let the fallow fields surrender
to the irretrievable.

Duck's Nest

She said when she was a little girl her best friend drowned. She watched the lifeguard squeeze the lake water out of her friend's lungs. He crouched over her and pushed against her body. He put his mouth over her mouth. She thought, how could this be a good thing? She said she did not grieve for her friend. What was her name, you ask. Veronica, yes, she was jealous of Veronica, wanted to change places. Not because everyone around wanted her to breathe again, but because she thought of the strange excitement of never waking up. *And what is my name? Why I'm the little girl, that's all.* She said her father would come into her bedroom, drunk, and breathe his stink into her mouth and push his cock into her, and, she said, she would wait for another day and then another night, until there was no difference between the two. And how she could not tell anyone, back then. How she never went back to that lake.

Cellmate

So much happens during sleep.
There's the boy who died from a drug overdose a long time ago.
And that one wave at Atlantic City that keeps washing ashore.
And the fence posts put in the ground to cordon off trespassers
who would sleep under the boardwalk after shooting up,
and how the wire was stretched from one post to the other
to give a finished look. How it never seems to get done.
The dream and all the work of the dream. The body, his body,
carried off in the dark to a morgue. And all the questions
his sister asks herself because she had said he wouldn't live
to see his twenty-first birthday, and how, maybe at this moment,
in her sleep, she is penned up and goes over and over the words
that won't let go.

Condemned

The prisoner sits on the cot in his cell.
Outside, if he could see outside,
he would see the perimeter fence
topped with concertina wire.
He would see the guard tower,
the haze in the distance,
the way it lies over the flatness of land.
He is reading the Bible. He is reading
the desert passages. Every thought
is a prison unto itself.
Prisoner No. T-72022 sits on the cot in his cell
and thinks about the immovable vessel
in which things are contained.
He is in two places.
After he stabbed to death
his estranged wife, their young son
and her thirteen-month-old daughter,
he ripped their hearts from their bodies.
In his cell there are no bars,
the walls are whitewashed,
the lighting fluorescent, almost blue;
then he plucks out his eye, he eats it.
There is no outside.

It Is Getting Dark

The wrong day, a fragile day, the sun so weak
through the haze, the heat like a blanket; the broken
day when a human heart was discovered
in his freezer. When skulls were uncovered
in his closet; an altar of candles. Corpses stored
in acid-filled vats. When the news media circled
in the afternoon. When the Lao family from the land
of a million elephants understood something
incomprehensible. In the shadow of the Oxford
Apartments in Milwaukee, a stray dog lifts
his hind leg and pisses on the cornerstone.
Then the glazed looks of the police. What is left
to say: the not-guilty plea by reason of insanity,
the subsequent conviction, the sentence of 957 years.
Then Dahmer, beaten with a barbell by an inmate
in the prison's gymnasium. Then his death. Then
some relief. Then a means to an end. Then I said,
Good, I'm glad he's dead. When maybe I should
feel some guilt. When. Maybe some wounds will not heal.
When. What can be more empty than loss; their eyes
dulled by drugs; their bodies raped and tortured.
Perhaps, a last plea. Perhaps he would not feed
on them. Perhaps he could let them go. A reminder
he still could feel. Perhaps then it is getting light.

Labor of Bells

In time everything bends;
out of the earth, a tree,
under each leaf, revelation.
Chandra was raped and murdered.
A man walking his dog, looking
for turtles in Rock Creek Park,
found her body. Always the underside
of things. What is the wheat without
the wind? Give us the breath
to revive her. Let her hear again
the labor of bells, lay bare
what is unspeakable.

Channel

A man walks to the midway point of a bridge.

He looks at the funnel of seawater below.

He looks at the gullet of the harbor in the distance.

There are white sailboats racing around Angel Island.

Departing is easier than meeting. He thinks when he hits the water

he will spread out like a net. His body will blend with the salt.

He thinks turning back would have the same result.

This is what he does: he holds his breath,

then tries to breathe normally.

Schuylkill

Sounds collected at day's end.
The last car of the light rail passed.
No one stood on the platform of the El.
No one saw the boxed light, the empty seats,
nor heard or saw anything. Of course this is not true.
When she was murdered...

Maybe we should not sleep anymore.
Maybe we should carry with us the terrible things
that happen. There is a river that winds
through this city; sometimes it seems to stop
but underneath, the river is awake.

Some News

A woman who was waiting for a bus after working a ten-hour shift at a counter-service diner was found beaten to death with a baseball bat, described on the eleven o'clock news as a blunt instrument. The motive of the assailant is unknown. The bus driver who arrived five minutes behind schedule said he didn't stop because he thought it was an old dog sleeping in its own shit. It's a little-known fact that most breeds of dog won't play fetch. If you throw a stick they'll look at you expectantly. The special at the café that night was chicken-fried something, instant mashed potatoes covered in white gravy, and a choice of okra or lima beans as a side dish, $6.99 plus. The police said she probably never knew what hit her. A witness said he thought he saw her waving one arm at the bus but couldn't be certain, seeing as it was pretty dark out.

Less Than Angels, More Than Machines

1982, Detroit

We haven't said a word. Almost simultaneously
we shake our heads over the lead story
about Vincent Chin, who was beaten
with a baseball bat by two unemployed auto workers.
They thought he was Japanese. He died four days later.
They have been given a light sentence: three years'
probation, a three thousand dollar fine, and seven
hundred and eighty dollars in court costs.
There's a snowstorm coming on, and we use
the newspaper to light the kindling; the logs
will catch fire. Our living room will warm up,
become almost comfortable again. We will live
in an opaque city, the serpentine river will freeze
and then later bleed again into blue, then green.

Grand Theatre

A man was punched in the face,
knocked to the ground, hit his head
on the concrete and dies a few days later.
The accused said he looked him in the eye
in a disrespectful way.
There should be no exceptions to mercy.

Forgive me, I sometimes lack compassion
for the guilty; sometimes I am not myself.

Existential

The roots of our lives are in the ground.

Yet we turn to the mechanics

of stars for answers, that they are somehow translatable.

For every truth there is an argument, the way people define

the dead by what they were not; murderers, no matter

their excuses or their manners are never kind or soft

spoken. I deny them this.

Death is the white winter of sleep.

Sleep heals temporarily. Ayn Rand said *existence exists*.

Non-existence is a bond impossible to break.

Only if left alone does it loosen its grip, the bare roots

exposed at the stream's edge. Of these things,

I can no longer say anything.

Define

Out of a lie, some truth. Out of a wound,
courage. From a scar, some history.
From history something learned and forgotten.
From insight, some sight. Out of fire, some ash.
Out of ash soap is made. From tallow comes lipstick.
From bone comes lime. From blood the worm
is nourished. Out of the Hebrew word for crimson
comes the worm. Out of suffering, strength. Out of sloth,
the virtue of rest. Out of cowardice some wisdom.
For everything that holds light, there is room
for darkness. In an immodest position,
some modesty shows. In every opinion,
some jealousy. Yellow and blue will always be
a part of green. A truism is the same
as disbelief. Everything depends on its angle.
Both sides being dependent.

Where Are You

Inside a house there's a family watching a pot boil.

Inside a beehive there's a queen who thinks she's a movie star.

Inside a cage there's a parrot that wants more than a cracker.

Inside a grammar school there are kids who want out.

Inside a restaurant there are sinners eating all the wrong foods.

Inside a church there are atheists.

Outside there are stray dogs and street people.

Outside there are talking birds perched on phone lines.

Outside there is a man with his hands in his pockets hurting,

there is rain in July, take-out food, drop-outs.

Outside there are drunks sleeping in their own piss,

they think they are sleeping *it* off.

Outside there are protestors stirring the kettle

while being filmed by the news media, and vultures circling

because they spy something dead

or almost dead.

Zazen

There is a wolf that stands alone in water.
The cause of death is the cause of life.

Everything in nature contains all there is in nature.
A hare stays still in the tall grass.

The Pawnee say: what is seen is temporary.
What is unseen shall not pass away.

Pahoo-Ka-Ta-Wah:
a wolf stands alone in water.

Pain Is About Damage

Bridge

Every life is measured. Yet it is impossible
to know a whole day. No moment is fixed.
The shadow of a hull and keel follows under
the water. The wake and drag follow.
Who doesn't suffer from absence?
Du Fu said it is better not to expect.
He also said, be careful, expect.
On the Grand Canal in Hangchow
he sat in the bow of a skiff, and passed
under a rainbow bridge toward banishment.
A singing girl along the bank
played a lute, her reflection
rippling.

Minder

After my friend Pat had a stroke,
aside from some physical manifestations,
she seemed to be her old self.
I dropped in on her one day
and she was pleased. She said
she had spent the whole week looking
for her jewelry box, when she discovered
the good doctors had put it inside her brain cage.
She was fingering something invisible to me.
When I asked her what she had in her hands,
she looked distressed and said it was a strand of pearls
that had belonged to her great-grandmother.
Pat raised her arms over her head as if to drape
a necklace around her neck; she smiled at me
and said she must remember to put it back
in that safe place that only she knew about.
Then it seemed she was looking through me.

Last Visit

for Evelyn Belvin

Who can predict the last of anything?
Somehow you walk into it and know.
For every room in her Tiburon apartment
was cluttered as though she were planning
to move. There was a blender and a toaster
in their original unopened containers
among books and magazines, and paper
shopping bags stacked under the window sill,
stuffed with what looked like sewing
machine parts. In the efficiency kitchen
reused mayonnaise jars, full and half-full,
of various kinds of tea or herbal blends,
and biscotti tins either empty or used
to store macaroni or dried beans and such.
She had water in a kettle on the stove
readying, on the counter two plates,
each with three cookies, each a different
kind; and she maneuvered her wheelchair
in this horseshoe space, the way a cowboy
would corral a steer, all the while freeing
herself of stray thoughts and poetry
she knew by heart, never finishing one line
before starting another. There was a look
of satisfaction on her face, and before I left
I watered her potted Meyer lemon tree
on the balcony she called her *grand lanai*.
The sun the way it is in mid-March, skimming
across the bay, the wind coming sideways,
the days longer already.

Hands to the Breastbone

When she looks around she sees a world without gaps,
so she assumes there must be a gap somewhere.
The aperture in the apse of a temple. The signs
that cannot be read in dreams. Blood congeals
below the skin. And she feels each bruise again.
It is the anchor. It is what holds. There can be
some beauty in the way flesh turns and deepens
to blue. Pain is about damage.
Healing, about repair.

Stray

She says she wants
a hairstyle that will make her look shorter,
says she wishes she could be someone else;
looks down at her feet dangling past the footrest
of the stylist's chair, puts her right hand across
her midriff as though she hungers. The ceiling
is ten feet from the floor. The overhead fan moves
the warm air downward. There she sits in
her body; it does not obey her. If she could travel
at the speed of light and then look in a mirror,
her image would not be there. Her whole space
would be diminished. To describe the end of someone,
draw nothing; this is not such a sad thing, it is just
something smaller. Perhaps there are fish that believe
they contain the sea. Who's to say that they don't?
The angels fell not because they were too small,
rather because their want was to be something greater.
For this their wings were torn from their bodies.

Interior

When you rubbed mud on your face
and arms to keep the mosquitoes
from biting, you believed this to be
a deception. There is something called
groundcover, scrub and brush,
that can shelter the living.
Because the things that stay hidden
are often in plain view. The wound
that goes into the body, the hurt
that is not from any cut.

Rope

A woman climbs over rocks that jut out in the harbor.
She loses her footing, then regains. There is so much danger
in living. This woman knows what she is risking.
She bears the injuries that have been inflicted upon her.
She believes that what her abusers have done to her
they have also done to themselves. She thinks
of Chinese calligraphers as they dip their brushes
into the inkpot to draw upon a rock face a rope of sand
or a perfect chrysanthemum. Something that can fall apart
but can also be held together in the mind.

About Pain

About a woman's pain
about why she is suffering and will not say why
she is suffering but the hurt is visible nonetheless
in her expression in the purchases she makes
at the farmer's market and in the canvas bag she carries
not because it looks one way or another but by the way
she carries that bag the way it struggles to leave her shoulder
it is difficult you see
                        nearby four children two boys & two girls
maybe seven years old maybe closer to ten
huddle around a barbecue pit
                          they are holding sticks
sticks that look torn from the witch hazel
they are roasting
                  what is it locusts? grasshoppers? who knows?
then they raise the charred critters to their lips
you can tell it burns their tongues
                         there is a sweetness
in the way they hold these tidbits there between their teeth
bitterness shows on their faces as the taste disappoints
these children move away
                  this is the way with pain
the way it must be consumed

The Hand

The hand can embrace and crush,
can mold and caress, can be held
or be like the clouds. The hand is vain
and corrupt, is kind and forgiving,
can draw on a canvas
something vast and beautiful,
can clear-cut a forest, strip a mountain.
Can hold a lie as stiffly as a rod
or truth as loosely as a string.

Shame

The heart knows how to do one thing well
but fails at so many others. It does not know
the number of bones in the body, or the number
of organs with their changing one thing into another,
or the way the skin gives everything away. Every part
is important to the whole, even the appendix,
even the little toe, even the fine hairs that cover the body.
Even the bare palms and the bare soles.

Blame

A woman lies on her bed alone.
The lights are out, the curtains drawn.
Perhaps a few gaps near the top
of the cornice lets in some reflection,
and occasionally the headlights
of a passing car search the drapes of her room,
then leave. The ceiling glows a dull white,
as though something of the day had been
trapped there. As though the woman who lies
on her bed alone had something to do with this.

Signs

From under the brim of a black umbrella,

you describe the celestial as an arcade

where a pinball game is being played out.

Where, no matter the skills of the players,

the steel balls are swallowed into a sinkhole.

We walk to your home looking down

at the slate sidewalk, tracking prints

to your front door. We don't look back because

we know what is already lost to us;

and then there's the next thing

we will touch upon

to think about.

Cause

A man is sitting in the dark in the room
he calls his study. He is alone, though he does
not feel alone. There is some light around
the cracks of the door, as though the door
were keeping something out. Thoughts come
in different shades, even in the dark, even in bright
daylight. Thoughts come even when the door
is closed, even when the man is sleeping.
The man is aware of the trouble he has caused
by being alone, by trying to study in the dark.

More

He crushed flowers for her because he loved her.
From the petals of marigold, lilac, and lavender
he extracted a perfume for her. She steeped for him
three herbs because she loved him. From the leaves
she extracted the essences of mint, savory, and marjoram.
The scent and taste. For someone sees
and someone listens.

Desire

And when desire leaves, you will feel
its passing, sharper than a sword
through the belly; you will remember
the taste on the back of the tongue,
hard water from a well, and you will say
three prayers, three times a day
for its return, but it will not return.
Just as before, desire does not bend
to the will.

Partnership

So much can be said about the compassion
the soul has for the body. The closeness
of the body overcomes the distance of the soul.
The wearing away.
And then the body leaves
the soul alone,
who was always watchful,
always wakeful.

The Wheat Field

Path to Migration

An old man in City Park is feeding the pigeons.
He is trying to teach them to be orderly and fair.
The pigeons will have none of this; they scramble
from one side of the park bench to the other
to gain advantage. If you would only be patient,
he says. And then his voice trails off. He is remembering
something from the Great War in Europe. Something
a historian would consider insignificant. One side or the other,
he says out loud. A girl was running out of a barn
in France, trying to save a chicken that had become frightened
by all the noise. A bullet went clear through her body;
she stood for a moment, then fell over. Now the old man's eyes
have a glassy look that could be angels closing in
around his vision. When a thought from the past fires the soul,
time is no more. Why won't you share? he says
to the pigeons.

Acres Divided

Today we will build a cemetery: the land will be laid out
in acres, the acres divided into grids, the grids broken down
into lots. Tombstones will be quarried out of granite, hauled
overland to the mill for the cutter to size and polish, to be
graded by color, sorted by weight, and stacked on straw
covered pallets until needed. The cemetery gardener will till
the land and sow the seed, tend and water the fescue, weed
and fertilize until called upon to cut and roll back the sod;
wield the digging bucket mounted on the back of a tractor,
using a two-jointed articulated arm to cut a hole in the earth.
He will tow the casket in a trailer, draped in our American flag;
the flag that holds the body, the body that will be buried
in this ground.

No Middle Name

His last name was stitched onto his jungle fatigues,
followed by his first initial,
about one inch above the left-side shirt pocket,
as though he were a little boy who might wander off
and become lost.
There were popping sounds in the distance,
the kind you would hear in a play
about gangsters.
The clouds that day were a fine art in their whiteness,
and from time to time they changed their shape and position.
And then there were voices,
as though coming from backstage, and laughter
as if someone had just told a joke;
they were coming toward us.
I wiped some grime off the soldier's cheek
with the back of my hand and swept his hair off his forehead.
He was so beautiful.
That's when I cursed out loud.
And then heard someone say, Over there,
it came from over there.

Infantryman (No Dog Tags)

I once put my mouth to another man's mouth
because he could not breathe on his own.
Blood rose from his throat, and I knew
there was nothing more to be done.
I depressed his tongue with my fingers
and turned his head to one side and let
what poured from him spread out
on the red dirt. I turned onto my back, lying
exhausted next to him. And held his hand
as his body cooled. The heat from the sun felt good,
but not the hunger not the shame.

Home Front

She tries to not think; tries the mind trick of writing
the problem on paper, then locking it away in a drawer.
The brain cannot be controlled. Arrogant muscle, she says
out loud. A friend suggested she make up a color
that doesn't exist. What doesn't exist? Who can avoid
hearing the news about those killed in action?
Even the public television channel gives her no comfort
when they broadcast the photos and vital statistics
without sound. She can't help thinking. Turning back
is a defeat, she's told. That could be said of friendly fire.
What does exist? A question.

Isolate

The wheat field, like ten thousand arms, and the dirt road
that cuts through the middle, the bisection. The tall flame
of the wheat, the height, the direction the dirt road takes —
like an arrow with a point and a tail on a map. One end leads
to another end, to a yellow farmhouse, to a split-rail fence
around the farmhouse in the middle of a wheat field, in the middle
of ten thousand arms. The dirt road, the yellow house and barn,
the red barn with the black oak, giving shade, taking light.
Everything anyone
could want.

Tourniquet

There is immensity. The sea with its own language
held together and not held together. And the heart
inside the body. Each keeps saying *don't stop.*
The burro circles, yoked to a pole turning the pump
to bring water up from the earth. There is a carrot
on the end of a stick. There is this thirst. But sometimes
he will not move. Even if prodded, the burro will not move.

Loss

There is knowledge and knowing,
there is order and there is giving
and taking. The flower obeys the laws
of nature, whether opening in full season
or the wilting in abandonment.
There is reason and choice.
What grieves is the knowledge.
It is what separates.

Vessel

A straw animal burned at the altar. Hibiscus
plucked from the topmost branch. Time and truth.
The sun sets on the Nine Pools, rises on Kunyu Mountain.
To the antelope, falling light renders the river visible.
Invisible light passing through prisms: light into color.
Each color attached. Blue into blue: ocean, bonnet, heaven.
Yellow into yellow: dandelion, lion's mane, wilt and field
of wheat. Red into red: color of heartbreak, remorse,
a red offering, millet, red millet, everywhere red is sown,
labor and harvest. Then the entrails of the ox are read,
then the fat burned for light, then the flesh consumed to sate hunger.
Red vessel of wood, of earthenware, vessel of ether, of light.

Ceremony

To scatter bread onto a body of still water, and wait
upon the mallards who partake of this offering, who gather
like the locusts who swarmed the Red Sea, who scooped up the leavings.
They make a sound like a kiss, muffled, the way someone
would pocket her lips in the palm of her hand to say goodbye
from a distance, a way of not letting go. And then to toss
a few coins into a wishing well and not tell what is hoped for,
what is given away in return.

About the Author

Photo by Margaretta K. Mitchell

Born in Newark, New Jersey, poetry came late to Joseph Zaccardi at the age of thirteen. His publications include *Vents* (Pancake Press 2005), *Render* (Poetic Matrix Press 2009), and *The Nine Gradations of Light* (Bark for Me Publications 2013). In 2003 he received an Individual Artist Grant from the Marin Arts Council, and in 2010 thru 2012 was editor of the Marin Poetry Center Anthology. He was appointed poet Laureate of Marin County, CA in 2013 for a two-year term. Since 1987 he has lived in Fairfax, tossing seeds from an imaginary apple tree.

Notes

"The Thing Lost"
Vinca is from the Latin to Bind, fetter. In India the plant is known as sadaphuli, meaning always *flowering*.

"Schuykill"
Schuykill is Dutch for hidden river. This river flows SE from E Pennsylvania to the Delaware River at Philadelphia.

"Lamb Wolf Farmer God You"
Jupiter, the chief god of the Roman state religion, originally known as the sky-god, was associated with thunder and lightning.

"Little"
Doughboy is an informal term for an American soldier, especially a member of the American Expeditionary Forces in World War 1. The term dates back to the Mexican-American War of 1846–48, after observers noticed U.S. infantry forces were constantly covered with chalky dust from marching through the dry terrain of northern Mexico, giving the men the appearance of unbaked dough, although this does not explain why only infantryman received the appellation.

Afterword

To write a single poem is a selfless act; to write a book of poems is a minor miracle. But miracles, minor or otherwise, don't happen by happenstance; they are engendered in part by hard work, in part by the generous help of others, and in part by inspiration and the drive to create. Therefore, this collection belongs not only to me, but also to those who gave unstintingly with their suggestions and nautical course corrections; and to that elusive *muse* poets have sought out for millennia.

The kick-off poem began at the Squaw Valley Writers Conference in the summer of 2010; the poem I wrote there, "Tied to Nothing," started my meanderings toward an undefined territory. I owe a debt of gratitude to those sixty-three poets sequestered with me in that valley. Six months later, that one poem had nineteen brothers and sisters, which I brought to a David St. John chapbook workshop as part of the Cloudview Poets, hosted by CB Follett and Susan Terris. One by one, sometimes by twos and threes, I shuttled more poems to my writers' groups: *Slash & Burn,* with poets Calvin Ahlgren, Sandy Scull, Phyllis Teplitz, and Sim Warkov; and the *Sophias,* with poets Rose Black, Donna L Emerson, and Janet Jennings. I'm indebted to all the poets in these groups and am grateful for their insights and refinements. I would also like to thank Yvonne Postelle, who agreed to write the foreword for *A Wolf Stands Alone in Water,* (not a small thing to do), and who went many steps further to steer me toward order in the chaos of sexual abuse, murder, and Alzheimer's; these poems of questions.

In this book there are things that belong to everyone, and there are things that should not belong to anyone. Such is the responsibility of the selfless act, and of poetry.

The typeface used throughout this book is *Dante* by Giovanni Mardersteig. The name comes from the first book in which it was first used, Boccaccio's *Trattatello in Laude di Dante*, published in 1955 by the Officina Bodoni. Dante would become one of the most used types by Mardersteig.

CPSIA information can be obtained
at www.ICGtesting.com
Printed in the USA
FSOW01n0538101115
13151FS

9 781625 491596